HISTORY FROM OBJECTS
AT
SCHOOL

Karen Bryant-Mole

Wayland

KT-539-429

HISTORY FROM OBJECTS

In The Home
Keeping Clean
At School
Toys
Clothes
In The Street

This edition published in 1996 by
Wayland (Publishers) Ltd

First published in 1994 by Wayland (Publishers) Ltd
61 Western Road, Hove, East Sussex, BN3 1JD, England

© Copyright 1994 Wayland (Publishers) Ltd

Edited by Deborah Elliott
Designed by Malcolm Walker

British Library Cataloguing in Publication Data
Bryant-Mole, Karen
  At School. - (History From Objects Series)
  I. Title II. Series
  370.9

HARDBACK ISBN 0-7502-1018-4

PAPERBACK ISBN 0-7502-1893-2

Typeset by Kudos Editorial and Design Services
Printed and bound by BPC Paulton Books Ltd

King's Road Primary School
Rosyth - Tel: 313470

Notes for parents and teachers

This book has been designed to be used on many different levels. It can be used as a means of comparing and contrasting objects from the past with those of the present. Differences between the objects can be identified. Such differences might include the shape, colour or size of the objects.

It can be used to look at the way designs have developed as our knowledge and technology have improved. Children can consider the similarities between the objects and look at the way particular design features have been refined. They can look at the materials that the objects are made from and the way they work. Modern goods are often made from modern materials such as plastic. Older mechanical objects are now frequently powered by electricity.

The book can be used to help place objects in chronological order and to help children understand that development in design corresponds with a progression through time.

It can also be used to make deductions about the way people in the past lived their lives. Children can think about how and why the objects might have been used and who might have used them.
It is designed to show children that historical objects can reveal much about the past. At the same time it links the past with the present by showing that many of the familiar objects we use today have their roots planted firmly in history.

Contents

Some of the more difficult words which appear in **bold** are explained in the glossary on page 30.

Pens

Pens are used for writing.

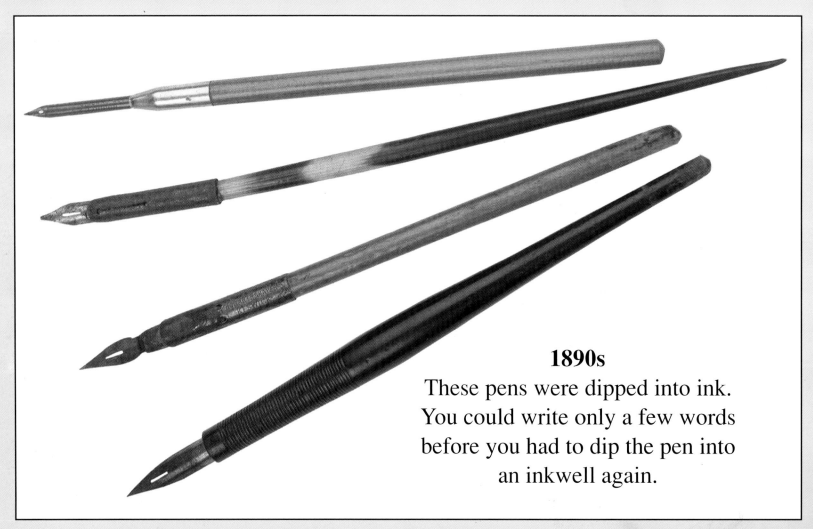

1890s
These pens were dipped into ink.
You could write only a few words
before you had to dip the pen into
an inkwell again.

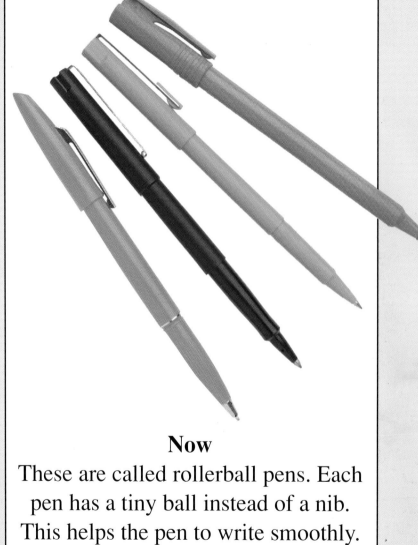

1950s

These pens stored ink inside them. One was filled by lifting the **lever** when the **nib** was in the bottle of ink. Another was filled by squeezing a rubber tube inside the pen.

Now

These are called rollerball pens. Each pen has a tiny ball instead of a nib. This helps the pen to write smoothly. You just throw the pen away when the ink has run out.

Colouring pencils

Colouring pencils are used for drawing pictures or colouring in pictures.

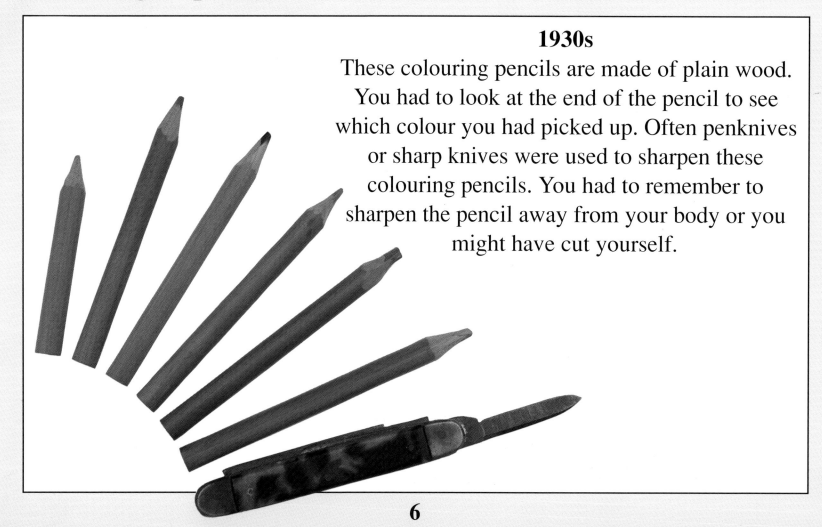

1930s

These colouring pencils are made of plain wood. You had to look at the end of the pencil to see which colour you had picked up. Often penknives or sharp knives were used to sharpen these colouring pencils. You had to remember to sharpen the pencil away from your body or you might have cut yourself.

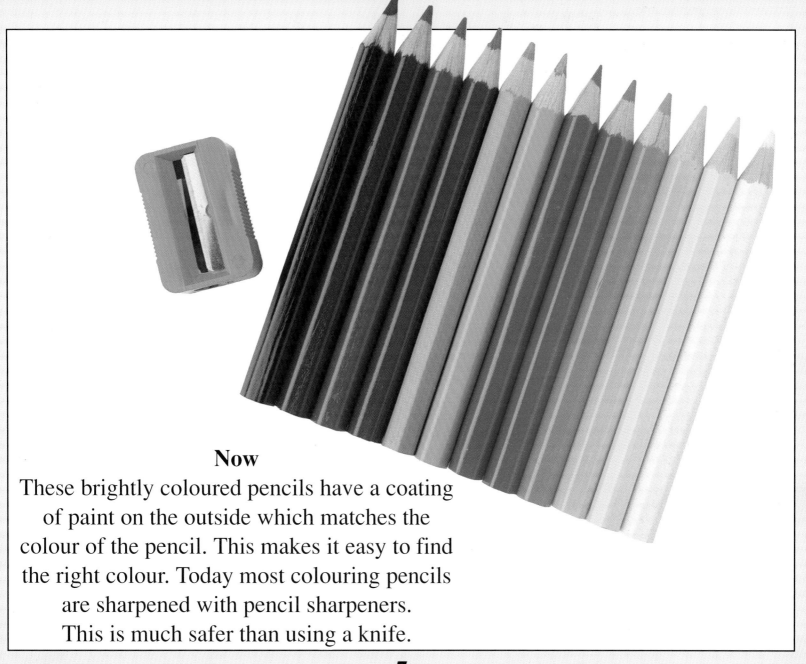

Now

These brightly coloured pencils have a coating
of paint on the outside which matches the
colour of the pencil. This makes it easy to find
the right colour. Today most colouring pencils
are sharpened with pencil sharpeners.
This is much safer than using a knife.

Work books

Children have always had to write their work down.

1880s

Children used to write their work on slates. Slates were a bit like little blackboards.

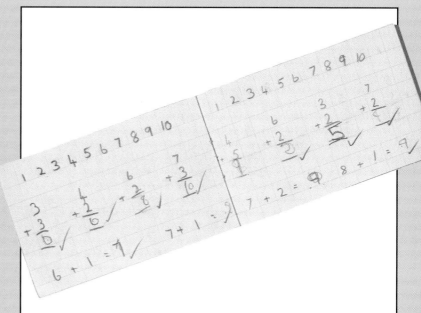

1960s

Children began to write in exercise books. They often had to write pages and pages of sums. Would you have enjoyed that?

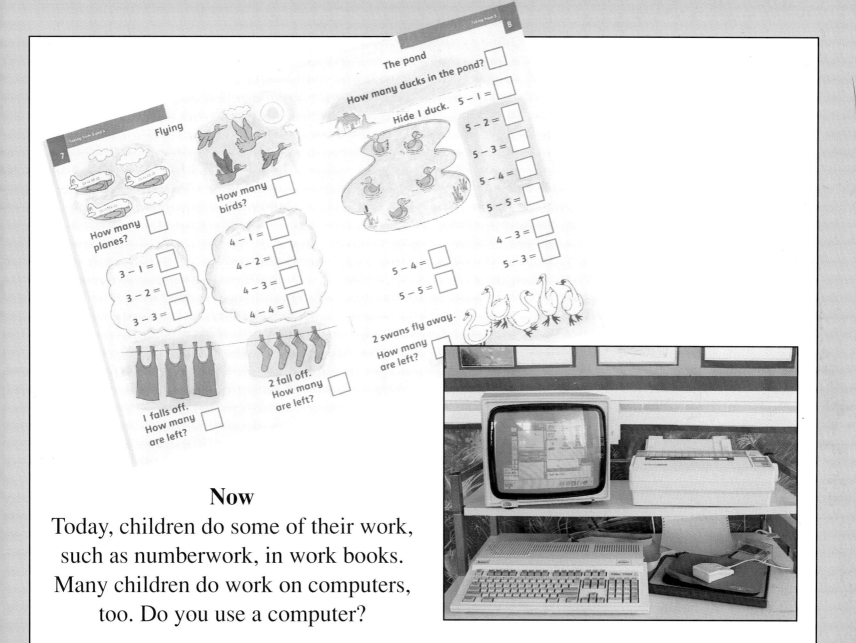

The pond

How many ducks in the pond?

Hide 1 duck.

$5 - 1 =$

$5 - 2 =$

$5 - 3 =$

$5 - 4 =$

$5 - 5 =$

$4 - 3 =$

$5 - 3 =$

$5 - 4 =$

$5 - 5 =$

Flying

How many
birds?

How many
planes?

$3 - 1 =$

$3 - 2 =$

$3 - 3 =$

$4 - 1 =$

$4 - 2 =$

$4 - 3 =$

$4 - 4 =$

1 falls off.
How many
are left?

2 fall off.
How many
are left?

2 swans fly away.
How many
are left?

Now
Today, children do some of their work,
such as numberwork, in work books.
Many children do work on computers,
too. Do you use a computer?

9

Text books

Books which tell you about a **subject** are sometimes called text books.

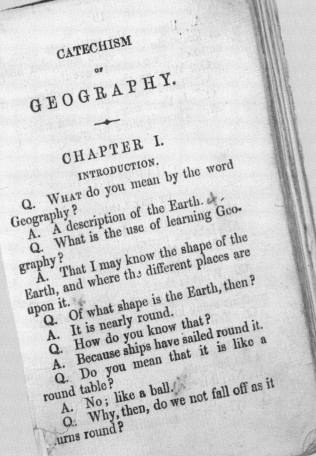

CATECHISM
OF
GEOGRAPHY.

CHAPTER I.

INTRODUCTION.

Q. WHAT do you mean by the word Geography?
A. A description of the Earth.
Q. What is the use of learning Geography?
A. That I may know the shape of the Earth, and where the different places are upon it.
Q. Of what shape is the Earth, then?
A. It is nearly round.
Q. How do you know that?
A. Because ships have sailed round it.
Q. Do you mean that it is like a round table?
A. No; like a ball.
Q. Why, then, do we not fall off as it turns round?

1900s

This is a geography text book. Children who used the book had to learn the answers to questions off by heart. There are no pictures in this book.

1910s

This geography book is a bit more friendly than the 1900s book. The way it was written is the way parents or teachers would talk to children. There are a few pictures in the book.

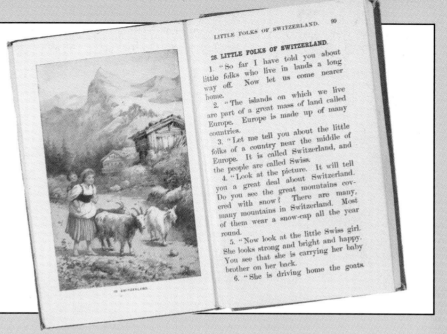

Now

This geography book is full of brightly coloured photographs. As well as giving facts, it shows ways of finding things out for yourself.

Reading books

Learning how to read is an important part of schoolwork.

1880s

This reading book has stories with lots of words which have the same ending. Some of the words, such as 'hog', are not used much today.

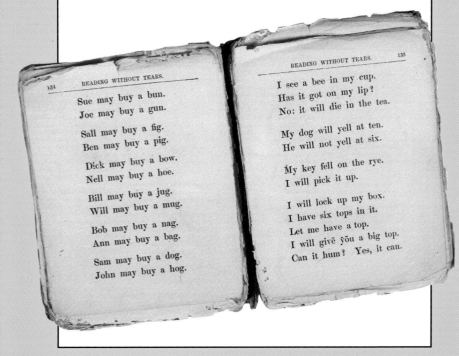

READING WITHOUT TEARS.

Sue may buy a bun.
Joe may buy a gun.

Sall may buy a fig.
Ben may buy a pig.

Dick may buy a bow.
Nell may buy a hoe.

Bill may buy a jug.
Will may buy a mug.

Bob may buy a nag.
Ann may buy a bag.

Sam may buy a dog.
John may buy a hog.

READING WITHOUT TEARS.   135

I see a bee in my cup.
Has it got on my lip?
No: it will die in the tea.

My dog will yell at ten.
He will not yell at six.

My key fell on the rye.
I will pick it up.

I will lock up my box.
I have six tops in it.
Let me have a top.
I will give you a big top.
Can it hum? Yes, it can.

82.

bog   log   hog
dog   fog   frog

Mildred and Winifred went into the glen and sat on a mossy bank.
"Let us sit very still, Mildred, and then the frogs will chat."

* * * *

The King of the Frogs sat on a log which was at the very edge of a bog.
Frogs Grumpy, Frisky and Sulky jumped sadly up to him.
The King wished them to tell him what was distressing them.

1900s

This reading book has a few colour pictures.

When John went home again
his little duck went too.
  Janet met John.
She looked at the little duck.
  "What do you call her?" she said.
  "I call her Little Fisher Duckling,"
John said.
  "She can dive under the water
and catch fish."

"What a clever little duck,"
said Janet.
  "We must take her to the pet show.
No one else will have a pet
like Little Fisher Duckling.
No one else will have a duck
that can catch fish.
Little Fisher Duckling must be there."

4

5

1950s

Ask your parents or grandparents if they used this book to learn to read. The book is part of a set of books called 'Janet and John'.

Now

Today there are lots of reading books to choose from. Some are part of a set of books. Others are just interesting, fun books with few words and lots of colourful pictures.

"Here is my house,"
said the cat.

15

Spot's Birthday Party

They went to the tree house.
Wilma wanted to make a video.

14

Dad let her use the camcorder.

AT SCHOOL Games

Games that teach you something are often called educational games.

1930s
This is a puzzle which, when it was completed, could show six different scenes from stories in the **Bible.**

1970s

This is a geography puzzle. When it was completed it showed all the countries of Europe and some north African countries. Since the puzzle was made some of the countries' names and **borders** have changed.

Now

Here is an alphabet puzzle. The pieces will only fit together if you find the letter that starts the name of the object in the picture. How well do you know the alphabet?

Satchels

Many children have a special bag for school.

1930s

This satchel is made of leather. It has two loops which you would have put your arms through. Other satchels had one long strap which went over your shoulder.

Now

Today, many children carry small rucksacks to school rather than satchels. Rucksacks come in lots of fun designs and colours. They might be used to carry a packed lunch, sports clothes or everyday things like pencils and crayons. What do you carry in your rucksack or bag?

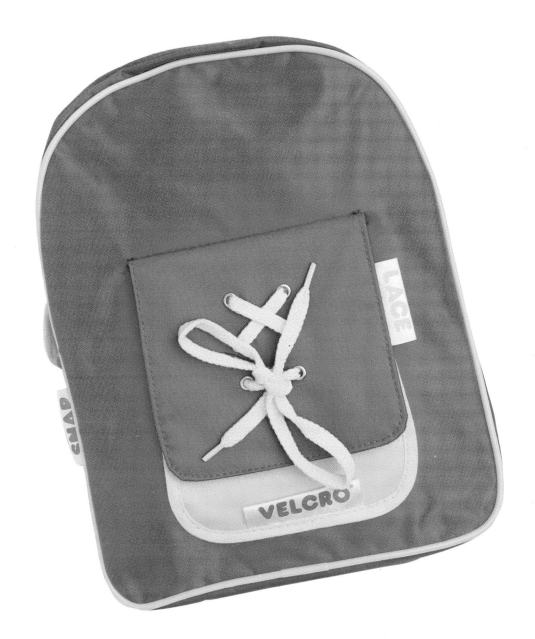

Pencil cases

Some children bring their own pencils and crayons to school in pencil cases.

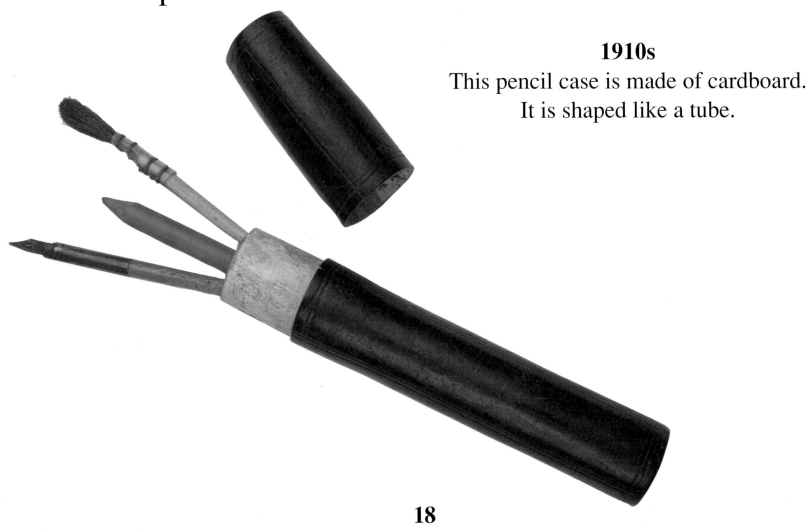

1910s
This pencil case is made of cardboard.
It is shaped like a tube.

1930s

This type of wooden pencil case was very popular for many years. It has two layers. To close the pencil case you had to swing the top layer shut and then slide the lid in and along.

Now

This pencil case is made of plastic. It has a plastic zip along the top, too. Today, pencil cases come in lots of different shapes, **materials** and colours. Many have pictures on them. Do you recognize the **character** on this pencil case?

Timetables

Teachers usually have a plan for each day which they write down as a timetable.

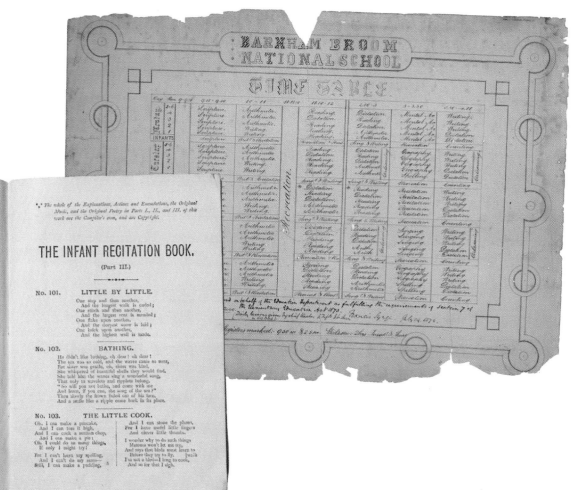

1870s

In the infant class at this school, each day started with **Scripture**. After this came writing and recitation. Recitation was saying poems out loud. Recreation, or play time, was followed either by more recreation and then reading, or by singing and writing. Each afternoon began with singing and writing, followed by recreation and counting.

May 14th

Theme: Living things — based around our chicks and eggs in the incubator.

Maths; Counting the number of unhatched eggs and comparing this with the number yesterday. Are there now more eggs or more chicks?
Adding the number of chicks born overnight to yesterday's total. Looking at the pattern of births and predicting the number of chicks tomorrow.

Science; Discussing the needs of the chicks — food, water, warmth. Relating this to caring for their own pets, including the fact that different pets need different food.

English; Describing the chicks both by sight and by touch. Making a list of appropriate words which could be used in written work.

Movement; Moving like animals eg. hopping like a rabbit, wriggling like a worm, moving slowly like a tortoise, jumping like a kangaroo, trotting like a horse etc.

Story; Spot Goes to the Farm — Eric Hill

Song; Old MacDonald Had a Farm.

Now

Most of today's infant classes do not have such a strict timetable.
Teachers have a topic or project for their class.
This means that each day's timetable might be different.
Often the only things that are fixed are play time, dinner time, hall time and, perhaps, assembly time.

Adding and subtracting

Adding and subtracting are used to work out sums.

1900s

These are different types of abacus. The abacus has been used as a way of adding and taking away for thousands of years. Beads were moved from side to side or up and down to work out the answers.

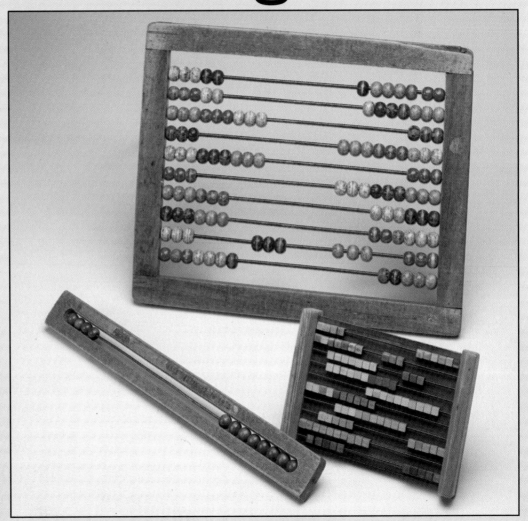

1960s

These are Cuisenaire Rods. The rods mean different numbers. The smaller the number, the shorter the rod. The greater the number, the longer the rod. Cuisenaire Rods can be used to add and subtract and are very useful for finding different ways of making the same number.

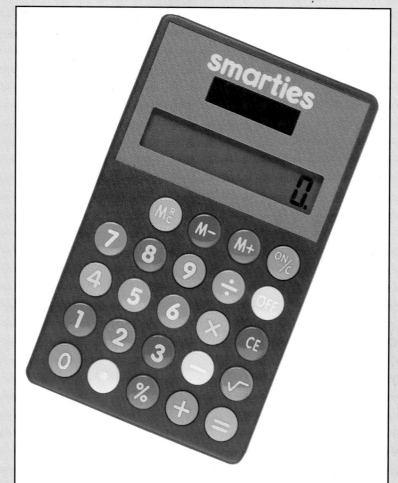

Now

This is a calculator. If you press the right buttons in order, the calculator will give you the answer to the sum.

Dinner time

In the middle of the school day everyone has lunch.

1950s
Before the **Second World War**, children used to go home at dinner time. After the war, dinners started to be cooked in schools. All the children could have a free, hot dinner. This meant that every child could have at least one good meal a day.

Now
Today many children bring a packed lunch to school in a lunchbox. Other children still prefer a hot dinner. This hot dinner might be cooked in the school kitchen, or it might be cooked somewhere else and brought to the school in a van.

The classroom

Most of the school day is spent in the classroom.

1890s

The wooden desks in this classroom are in straight rows. They all face the front of the class. There was no electricity in the classroom. The room was lit by gas lamps which you can see at the top of the picture. There were about sixty children in this class. The room looks very crowded, doesn't it?

Now

There are fewer children in this classroom and there is more space.
The children sit on plastic chairs around low tables.
There is a carpet on the floor instead of bare floorboards.
The children are doing lots of different things

The playground

At play time you have fun in the playground.

1930s

This playground looks very bare. There was nothing for the children to play with, so they made up their own games, like catch, clapping games and rhyming games. These children are playing a game called 'Ring-a-Roses'.

Now

This playground looks much more fun. There is a game marked out on the ground. What game do you think the children are playing? It is hopscotch.

Glossary

Bible   a holy book used by people who believe in the Christian religion

borders   the edges of something

character   someone in a play or story, or in a television programme

lever   something which is pushed or pulled

materials   what things are made of

nib   the point of a pen, used to write

Scripture   the holy writings of a religion

Second World War   the war fought in Europe from 1939 until 1945

subject   a topic to learn about, such as history or geography

1850 S	1860 S	1870 S	1880 S	1890 S	1900 S	1910 S	1920 S

Books to read

History From Photographs series by Kath Cox and Pat Hughes (Wayland, 1995-6)
How We Used To Live, 1902-1926 by Freda Kelsall (A & C Black, 1985)
How We Used To Live, 1954-1970 by Freda Kelsall (A & C Black, 1987)
People Through History series by Karen Bryant-Mole (Wayland, 1996)
Starting History series by Stewart Ross (Wayland, 1991)

The illustration below is a timeline. The black and white drawings are of all the objects you have seen photographed in this book. Use the timeline to work out which objects came earlier or later than others, and which were around at the same time.

1930 S	1940 S	1950 S	1960 S	1970 S	1980 S	NOW

Index

Fife ⋆⋆
C O U N C I L
King's Road Primary School
Rosyth - Tel: 313470

Acknowledgements
The Publishers would like to thank the following organizations, which supplied the objects used in this book: Beamish Photographic Library 26; By courtesy of the Royal Pavilion, Art Gallery and Museums, Brighton 4, 6, 8 (left), 10, 12 (left), 18, 19 (left), 20: Norfolk Museum Services 14, 20, 22. All photographs are by Zul Mukhida except: pages 14, 20, 22 which are by GGS Photographic ; pages 9 and 27 which are by APM Photographic; pages 24 and 28 which are supplied by Hulton Deutsch Collection Limited and pages 25 and 29 which are supplied by the Wayland Picture Library.